The Eudaimonic Rhythm

by Sulien Valentino Solovyov

The Eudaimonic Rhythm
by Sulien Valentino Solovyov

ISBN: 978-1-989647-79-0
First published October 6, 2025
Toronto, Canada

Publisher: The Evergreen Center

Publisher's Cataloging-in-Publication Data
Solovyov, Sulien Valentino.
    The Eudaimonic Rhythm : A System for Integrated Growth and Deep Fulfillment / Sulien Valentino Solovyov. — First edition.
    Summary: An anti-nihilistic guide that presents The Eudaimonic Rhythm, a philosophical system integrating ancient virtue ethics with modern concerns about burnout and digital fragmentation. It introduces a two-phase cycle—the Effort Cycle and the Fallow Cycle—as a practical structure for achieving deep fulfillment and cultivating meaning, presented through aphorisms, stories, and poetry.
    Identifiers: ISBN 978-1-989647-79-0
    Subjects: Philosophy—Ethics. | Eudaimonia. | Virtue Ethics. | Self-Help—Time Management. | Anti-Nihilism. | Personal Growth—Rhythm.
    Classification: 170.4—dc23 (Dewey Decimal Classification for Practical Philosophy / Applied Ethics)

The Eudaimonic Rhythm

by Sulien Valentino Solovyov

The Eudaimonic Rhythm: A System for Integrated Growth & Well-being

This system is grounded in a profound insight: lasting personal growth and deep fulfillment—Eudaimonia—doesn't come from endless striving, but from a dynamic, intentional balance. It's a structured rhythm of focused effort, deliberate learning, strategic rest, and meaningful connection. Think of it as "Interval Training for Life"—a powerful, sustainable approach designed to prevent burnout while unlocking your long-term potential for a life well-lived.

Core Principles

Life as Skill & Virtue Acquisition: Every aspect of life—from practical hobbies to inner character traits—can be shaped and refined through intentional, consistent practice.

Growth as a Cycle, Not a Climb: True development unfolds in sustainable rhythms—periods of effort followed by renewal and integration—not as a relentless ascent.

Deliberate Rest as Formation: Rest isn't passive escape; it's essential to growth. Think of it as a fallow cycle—a quiet, fertile time for integration, renewal, and receptivity.

Purpose Beyond Performance: The goal isn't just achievement, but the cultivation of a meaningful, virtuous, and deeply fulfilling life—what Aristotle and the ancients called Eudaimonia.

Community as Catalyst & Context: Shared effort and shared rest amplify individual growth and rebuild a fractured social fabric. They're not extras; they're essential.

The Eudaimonic Cycle: Core Phases
Phase 1: The Effort Cycle (Focused Growth & Contribution)

This is a period of intentional striving—actively engaging in skill development, character cultivation, and meaningful contribution.

Examples:

Mastery Skills: Baking a complex bread recipe, constructing a Raspberry Pi system, tending an heirloom garden, learning a musical scale, or practicing Qigong forms.

Virtuous Practices: Choosing patience in difficulty, performing intentional service, practicing forgiveness, or committing to contemplative prayer or mindfulness.

Community Engagement: Joining a group project, organizing an event, or volunteering (e.g., coding for a non-profit, contributing to a permaculture initiative).

Duration: Continue until you reach productive fatigue—that natural signal of mental, physical, or emotional depletion. This is not a failure point—it's the healthy boundary that signals it's time to step back.

Purpose: To drive growth, sharpen character, and make real contributions.

The Eudaimonic Cycle: Core Phases
Phase 2: The Fallow Cycle (Rest, Integration & Rebalancing)

This is a conscious, deliberate disengagement from intensity.

It's a necessary pause for replenishment, quiet receptivity, and holistic recalibration.

Examples:

Solo Replenishment: Silent nature walks, sipping tea without distraction, journaling freely, listening to music for pleasure, or gentle stretching without a goal.

Communal Restoration: Sharing a slow meal, laughing with friends, or sitting together in a relaxed, agenda-free setting. No performance. Just presence.

Purpose:

Deep Recovery: Physical, emotional, and cognitive replenishment.

Integration: Allowing new insights and habits to settle in and become part of you.

Burnout Prevention: Respecting limits before exhaustion takes hold.

Cultivating Contemplation: Making space for inner quiet, imagination, and joy—what Josef Pieper called the basis of true culture.

Duration: As long as needed for genuine restoration—until you feel re-centered and whole.

Why This Framework Resonates Today

This rhythm speaks directly to the challenges of modern life—especially for younger generations navigating burnout, digital fragmentation, and spiritual hunger.

A Ritual Against the Attention Economy: Reclaims presence from endless scrolls and alerts; reorients life around depth, not distraction.

A Return to the Tangible: Prioritizes hands-on skills, nature, and real-world connection over abstraction and screen time.

Clear Structure, Not Vague Advice: Offers a usable rhythm—effort, rest, renew—instead of platitudes.

Rest is Required: Undermines hustle culture by making rest not a retreat, but a vital phase of growth.

Growth is Learnable, Not Mystical: Demystifies virtue and character development—turning aspiration into action.

Builds Emotional Intelligence: Encourages awareness of limits and needs through recognition of "productive fatigue."

Promotes Resilient Living: Embeds recovery into growth, creating long-term strength instead of short-term surges.

Validates All Arenas of Life: Recognizes that growth happens everywhere—kitchens, gardens, prayer, relationships—not just at work.

Combats Isolation: Anchors personal growth in shared rhythms of rest and contribution.

Centers Purpose Over Performance: Shifts the focus from achievement addiction to meaningful, intentional living.

Softens Perfectionism: Embraces cyclical, nonlinear progress. You don't have to be "on" all the time to be moving forward.

A Brief Guide to Implementation

The Eudaimonic Rhythm is a philosophical framework, not a third schedule to keep. It requires intention, not more time. Your objective is simply to decide what belongs in the two schedules you already have: the time for intentional striving and the time for deliberate rest.

1. Defining Your Cycles

The first step is to recognize and respect your own natural rhythm. The length of the **Effort Cycle** and **Fallow Cycle** is adaptive and non-prescriptive—it may last a day, a week, or a season—but the boundary between them must be intentional.

The Effort Cycle is your time for Intentional Striving. Its purpose is Skill Acquisition & Virtue Cultivation, focusing on input and production. You know to stop when you reach Productive Fatigue: the healthy limit where focus fades and performance turns brittle.

The Fallow Cycle is your time for Deliberate Disengagement. Its purpose is Deep Recovery, Integration, and Receptivity—a conscious cessation of output. You know this cycle is complete when you feel Restored Wholeness: a sense of centeredness, presence, and renewed energy for contribution.

2. Weaving in the Core Disciplines

The foundational disciplines are the tools that translate the philosophy into action.

During the Effort Cycle, focus on disciplines that involve the hands and the will. Practice Sacred Craft & Devotional Labor by dedicating focused time to hands-on making—whether coding, gardening, or baking—without distraction. Simultaneously, dedicate yourself to Virtue Practice by choosing one character trait (like patience or fortitude) to intentionally cultivate in moments of daily friction.

During the Fallow Cycle, focus on disciplines that open the self to the world. Practice Deep Listening and Fallow Journaling by engaging the world without commentary, listening to nature, observing people, and recording unrooted, quiet thoughts. You may also employ Phenology & Awareness by observing and recording small changes in your local environment, connecting your internal rhythm to the slow, steady one of nature.

3. Instituting The Sacred Pause

The transition point between the Effort and Fallow Cycles is the most critical part of the system. This pause must be a conscious break, not a collapse into distraction.

To initiate the Fallow Cycle, establish a Linger-Spot: designate a chair, a doorstep, or a window as a place dedicated solely to being without purpose. Commit five to ten minutes in this spot to actively choose disengagement.

To conclude the Fallow Cycle and begin a new Effort Cycle, use a structured pause—Three Deep Breaths. These slow, intentional inhalations and exhalations clear the mind of the previous phase's residue and allow you to set a clear, conscious intention for the next. This ensures you are not merely defaulting to the next task, but actively choosing it.

The Rhythm is not complicated. It is simply about giving your attention and energy to two things: what you are building and what you are allowing to integrate. **The**

Rhythm Embodied

It is vitally important to have a system's framework—the rules, the cycles, and the tools. But a philosophy is only as durable as its expression in the chaos of life.

The structure of the book that follows reflects the Rhythm itself: a deliberate alternation between Effort and Fallow. The coming sections do not offer instruction, but Imitation.

You will encounter:

- **Stories,** ordinary and fantastic, of players working with and through the elements of this system;
- **Aphorisms** distilled from decades of trial and err, of observation and labor.
- **Poetry** that uses silence, space, and rhythm to embody the quiet work of integration.

These pieces are the Case Studies of Eudaimonia. They are presented not as grand answers, but as fragmented mirrors reflecting the constant, humble, anti-nihilistic work of finding meaning in the simple act of showing up.

They invite you to use the Fallow Cycle for integration, allowing these small moments of insight to take root in your own silent attention.

In Closing

This system doesn't promise a flawless life—it offers something better: a rhythm for real flourishing. The Eudaimonic Rhythm is a way to bring sanity to ambition, humanity to hustle, and meaning to motion. It's not about chasing constant progress—it's about living with integrity, presence, and joy through a cycle that honors both effort and rest.

A life well-lived isn't built in one mode. It breathes. It balances. It grows.

Welcome to the Rhythm.

Section I: The Rhythm Beneath All Things
Discipline: Deep Listening & Sonic Ecology

Rooted in Yolŋu Aboriginal songlines, Benedictine obsculta ("listen with the ear of the heart"), and practices like acoustic ecology and soundwalking, deep listening is the foundation of a eudaimonic life.

It attunes us to the world's rhythms—wind, breath, silence—shaping our attention and presence.

By listening deliberately, we ground ourselves in the cycle of effort and rest, preparing for meaningful action.

The Shepherd Who Heard the Stones Breathe

There was once a shepherd who spent his years in the
high hills, far from the village road. He was not especially
devout, nor very talkative. His flock was small, his coat
mended many times, and his dog an old, lopsided thing
with one good ear.

In the beginning, he muttered to himself out of boredom,
or counted the sheep again when fog rolled in. But after
enough seasons had passed, the silence around him began
to change.

He noticed that certain stones clicked faintly before dusk,
like teeth settling in a jaw. Others gave off a low hum when
the sun struck them at the right angle. The wind through a
dead tree sang a minor chord. And before storms, the crows
would fall quiet, and the moss would seem to breathe.

One night, near midwinter, the silence came so thick
it seemed to press on his ribs. He did not sleep. He sat
upright on his cloak, his hand resting on a wooden bowl
he'd carved years ago to catch rain.

In the morning, the sky was clear, and he stood up slowly,
as if older. He returned to his flock and did not speak of it.

When he came down from the hills for good, he settled in
a small cottage near the chapel. He kept no animals, but
sometimes took bread to the widow next door. He spoke
little, but when he did, people said it was like a bell rung in
fog—soft, but hard to ignore.

When he died, they found the wooden bowl on the
windowsill, polished smooth by his hands. Some said it
caught sound. Others said it had once held the rhythm of
the world.

No one could prove either. But on cold mornings, the
villagers sometimes found it filled with dew, even when
the other windows were dry.

On Listening as Praxis

Hearing happens; listening is a choice.

Sound is presence, not noise.

The world speaks to those who
pause.

You can't hear rhythm without finding your own.

Deep listening reshapes the listener.

       Silence hums

when you slow to meet it.

Truth stirs before   it speaks.

       Every place has a pulse—listening finds it.

Attention is the root

of understanding.

       To listen

is

 to stand

still

and be

changed.

Tidepooling

Arrived just after the moon had pulled the sea back.
Slick mirror left behind. Tidal pool, 4pm PST. Four days
out. Boots soaked and insufficient but miles to cover.
Crouched beside a still pool. Legs aching. Mist turning to
rain. Finally: a single crab. One. In ninety minutes. Shifted
just as I was planning to stand and walk back to the car.
Crab paused mid-step. Barnacles clicked softly in their
sleep. No answers. Two animals looking at each other.
Both wary. Neither hurried.

tide gone / a heron's beak taps / its own reflection

twig snapping time
it's dusk and there are items to wash and fold
bedclothes
pants
shirts with stains and
shorts that somehow are still around
in
tatters and
waiting for a threaded care

fireflies
silent
lanterning
to me

chores need
attention

do they call it pineconing if you are looking for
the perfect one

Section II: Effort as Offering
Discipline: Sacred Craft & Devotional Labor

Drawing from Benedictine *ora et labora* (prayer and work)
and Japanese *shokunin kishitsu* (artisan spirit), every task—
however small—becomes a path to meaning within the
eudaimonic cycle.

Offering effort with intention transforms work into a vessel
for presence, gratitude, and growth, shaping both the doer
and the done.

The Bricklayer's Prayer

In a hill town with narrow streets and yellow dust, a boy was apprenticed to a temple mason. His job was simple: lay bricks for the outer courtyard wall. It was unglamorous work—long rows, low pay, no blessing spoken over the labor.

The master mason never came to check. Only the old stonemason, who worked nearby, would sometimes glance over. One afternoon, without looking up, the old man said:

"Lay each brick as if it will outlast you. Whether anyone sees it or not."

The boy kept working. The days were hot. Years passed, and he moved on—to roads, houses, and finally bridges. He forgot the names of his early works.

Decades later, travelers coming to the temple often paused in that courtyard. There was nothing remarkable about the wall, but people slowed down near it. They spoke more quietly. Some even said they felt as if the place was listening.

No plaque bore a name. No record marked the boy's labor.

But when someone once asked the old stonemason, who still swept the steps in the late afternoon, he nodded and said:

"What you do when no one sees becomes what others feel when they arrive."

On Devotional Labor

Craft is care made visible through repetition.

Excellence without witness is still a gift.

What the hand repeats, the heart begins to know.

Not all altars are grand—some are swept floors, mended tools, folded cloth.

Tools don't make work meaningful—presence does.

Small tasks, done well, shape the doer.

Effort offered freely becomes its own reward.

The mundane, attended to, reveals the profound.

Work with attention builds more than objects.

Every finished task leaves a mark on the soul.

Gardening (After Harvest)

Frost last night. Tomatoes turned. Compost steam rising in the blue light. Cleared the last of the beans, stems brittle. Left the roots. Earth doesn't mind. Quiet digging. A worm curled around my finger—alive, warm. Took that as a good sign. Neighbor's dog barked once, then silence.

final picking / one overripe plum / splits in my hand

Section III: Cycles of Becoming
Discipline: Phenology & Seasonal
Awareness

Rooted in traditional planting calendars, lunar gardening, the Wheel of the Year, and the ecological study of phenology, this discipline teaches that growth follows natural cycles.

Like the moon or tide, human effort ebbs and flows—visible in some seasons, hidden in others.

The Personal Planting Chart helps map these rhythms, not to maximize yield but to honor both blossom and dormancy.

The Gardener Who Stopped Forcing the Bloom

There once was a gardener who believed that beauty must never rest. She coaxed her flowers to bloom through every season. When the sun faded, she lit glass domes with artificial light. When the earth cooled, she warmed the roots with wires. She fed the soil constant nutrients, rushing the cycle. And bloom they did—lavish, luminous, unrelenting.

But the blossoms came at a cost. Their roots grew shallow, their stems brittle. The scent faded early. By the third year, the soil had hardened. The plants, exhausted, gave nothing more. One by one, they collapsed under their own weight. The gardener, watching her garden fall silent, felt something in herself go quiet too.

Nearby, beyond the hedgerow, an old man tended a quieter plot. He rose with the sun and slept with the dusk. He touched the soil with his bare hands and smelled the air before planting. His garden was never early, rarely showy, and sometimes barren in winter. But when it bloomed, it held.

Intrigued, the gardener came to watch. The man did not teach with words. He let her carry the watering can, let her prune a vine too early, let her scatter seeds just a bit too soon. She saw how he waited—not lazily, but attentively. How he spoke to the wind before digging. How he knew the difference between dormancy and death.

So she went home and dismantled the domes. She let the soil go dark and undisturbed. The first season passed in silence. The second brought weeds. But the third—on an unremarkable morning in early spring—brought a single crocus. It bloomed crooked, low to the ground, its purple soft as breath. But it was true.

She knelt beside it, hands in the living dirt. That small bloom, earned through waiting and care, meant more than all the perfect flowers she had once forced into being.

on Cycles, Timing, and Letting Go of Linear Progress

Growth spirals, not climbs.

Fallow time builds roots unseen.

No tree blooms always—nor should you.

The moon wanes without apology.

Some lessons arrive only through waiting.

Wintering is not wasted time.

Feel the weather in your bones before planning.

Ripening resists haste.

Cycles teach what straight lines cannot.

Rest is growth's quiet partner.

Stacking Stones

Creek high from last night's rain. Took an hour to find three stones that agreed. None flat. No talking. Set them, watched for tremble. None. Took a photo, deleted it. Let the water reclaim.

stream carries / a single leaf upward / into the wind

Section IV: The Sacred Pause
Discipline: Natural History Wandering & Field Sketching

This practice draws from Victorian rambling, Muir's sauntering, and modern nature journaling. It slows perception to reveal overlooked details.

The Sacred Pause is not about knowledge collection, but about becoming porous to the more-than-human world.

The Linger-Spot—a chosen patch of earth—becomes a quiet teacher of time and presence.

The Town That Outlawed Rest

In a town hemmed in by ticking clocks, the people did not pause.

Their shoes were engineered for speed. Meetings were stacked like crates. Even trees were trimmed at regular intervals so that no branch dared surprise the light. Children learned to recite facts while walking briskly. Elders learned to sit in motion—fidgeting fingers, bouncing heels, eyes always scanning.

Stillness, in time, became a kind of crime—not by law, but by shame. To linger was to waste. To pause was to fall behind.

But on the edge of this town, beyond the final bus stop, a stream bent itself into a question mark. No one noticed it. Its waters passed in silence, its banks unkempt, its reeds disobedient.

One evening, a woman who had once been punctual, respected, and weary found herself standing beside that crooked water. Her legs, unbidden, folded beneath her. She sat.

No task accompanied her. She held no phone. The sky deepened. A snail, no larger than a coin, traced an invisible story across her shoe. A heron unfolded from the reeds like paper, stepped once into light, and vanished.

She felt herself dissolve—not into sleep, but into awareness.

When she returned to the town, her gait was different. She no longer filled silences. She looked at things longer than necessary. People noticed. They whispered.

She did not explain.

But the change was contagious. One by one, others began slipping away—to alleys, to benches, to quiet thresholds. Some returned with pockets full of leaves they hadn't meant to pick up. Others came back with poems. A child brought a feather longer than his arm and said only, "It was floating."

Years passed. The town did not collapse. Commerce continued. But something shifted.

One spring, without much debate, a new civic ordinance was quietly passed. It read:

"Each citizen shall keep a spot that asks nothing of them."

And though no one enforced it, most obeyed.

Somewhere, beyond the town's noise, the stream kept curving.

Not all paths need a destination.

on Fallow Time, Slowness, and Attentive Presence

A pause invites, it doesn't empty.

Lichen grows slowly but maps the wind.

Attention speaks louder than words.

Stillness hums with unnoticed life.

Rushing blinds you to the world's pulse.

Observing is a quiet act of care.

Tread lightly—everything converses.

You're not behind, just where the tide rests.

Lingering reveals what haste conceals.

Section V: Practices of Integration
Discipline: Fallow Journaling & Monastic Anchors

Drawing from cloister and zendo traditions, this practice clears space for inner composting. Not all meaning arises fully formed. The Fallow Book—a sparse, unstructured journal—becomes a container for fragments, half-seeds, and questions not ready to be answered.

The Fallow Book
A journal with no agenda.
No goals or insights.
A slow field.

fleeting thoughts

        stray images

dreams

        unread books - waiting

        wildlife sightings

moments that linger.

Carry a small object—stone, shell, ribbon—touch it when
something stirs.

Do not reread too soon. Let entries lie fallow.

The Apprentice and the Stone

An apprentice once asked his teacher,

"How will I know what matters?"

She said nothing, but placed a small stone in his palm—warm from her hand, ordinary to the eye.

"Carry this," she said. "Each time the world stirs something in you—curiosity, sorrow, delight—touch it. Don't name the feeling. Just mark it."

He carried the stone.

When the wind unsettled him, he touched it.

When music caught at something he could not speak, he touched it.

When he laughed and didn't know why, he touched it.

Seasons passed. He never spoke of the stone. He never showed it to others. But slowly, he began to listen more. Not to answers, but to thresholds. Half-formed thoughts. Feelings without roots. The stone anchored nothing. But it accompanied everything.

One morning, under the hush of winter branches, he reached into his pocket—and found the stone gone.

Panic flickered—then stilled.

He looked out across the frost-laced field.

A bird passed overhead, silent.

He let the moment rise. And fall.

Something in him recognized the shape of it.

He walked on, hands empty, no longer needing the stone.

He had become the field that could hold the stirring.

Listening to Geese

Woke before the light. Sound came before sky—high, layered, moving. Then the shapes: V-formed and loose. Flocks broke, reformed, tilted south.

One bird flying slightly behind, always slightly behind.

sky bare again, but / a feather spins / then settles

Washing the Bowl

Meal done. Silence full. Washed the single bowl with cold water and lye soap. Dried it with a cloth that smelled of sunlight. Set it in its place, exactly.

evening bell / one breath held / before it fades

Section VI: Inner Character, Outer Life
Discipline: Virtue Practice & Reflective
Self-Cultivation

Drawing from Stoic ethics, monastic self-examination, and Franklin's virtue charts, this practice treats character as a steady discipline.

Rather than posturing or purity, it focuses on small, habitual acts that form inner structure.

The House of Quiet Mirrors

A man once lived in a house filled with mirrors.

He hadn't meant to collect them—but over the years, they gathered: above the sink, near the door, in the corner where he practiced speeches he'd never give. Each one showed a different version of himself—charming, careful, clever, composed.

One day, after a long illness, he stopped looking.

Instead, each morning, he opened a small notebook and wrote a single word to carry through the day—temperance, honesty, fortitude. The words were modest, and so were his acts: waiting without complaint, admitting when he was wrong, helping someone without needing to be seen.

Seasons passed. Dust gathered. The mirrors slowly lost their shine. Not broken, just softened—like winter windows or old pond glass. In them, faces still flickered, but not sharply. The reflections no longer demanded to be believed.

Visitors noticed the change, though they couldn't say why.

"He seems different," they said. "Calmer. Easier to be around."

They didn't mention the mirrors.

One spring, he moved a chair near the garden door, where the light fell just right.

In the evening, he would sit with his notebook, a cup of tea, and the mirror across from him—now cloudy, gentle, and almost kind.

He didn't need it to show him who he was.

It was enough to be still, and true, and quiet in his own company.

Fox & Beans

Working the dry dirt—tending the last row of
late-season beet greens. Quiet work. The kind
that settles the mind like cold river silt.

Then the shadow moves.

From the tangled mess of alder and blackberry,
the Fox steps out. Not in a rush, not spooked.
She owns the woodshed, owns the thicket,
owns the space between the rows. Just moving,
knowing the ground, the Way of the place.

Behind her, the small one. Lagging.
Could be old age. Could be a sprung trap in the
deep woods somewhere else. Doesn't matter,
not my business.
They settle down by the edge of the dried-out
bean stalks.

No sound. No call. No names spoken.
Just the damp air and the falling light.
A shared stretch of the moment. We breathe,
they sit.
The transaction is complete. The exchange is
registered.

Beet greens
brushed by the low belly of the lame one
not mine
not mine, anymore
and that's the Law.

Impossible Possum

Impossible
O
possum
Sneak and peak and check the barrel
Round the fence in steady gate and
Ugly visage plodding nighttime roundabouts
Carry all your children on the run
From backyard lights
Spying on the bats and wondering about
their flight
Waddling hunting scurry grip and climb and
hurry
Possum
You are a poor-eyed treasure
In my mind

on Character Practice

Virtue is practiced, not posed.

Character grows from daily
choices, not grand gestures.

Quiet virtue builds
unshakable foundations.

Reflection without action
is empty; action without
reflection is blind.

Small habits shape the soul's
architecture.

Fallibility is part of the path—
return is the practice.

Honest self-accounting
reveals growth's gaps.

The goal is presence, not
perfection.

Each choice carves a deeper
channel for virtue.

Live the virtue you seek, and
it becomes you.

Section VII: Community as Rhythm
Discipline: Permaculture & Communal
Stewardship

Rooted in Indigenous land stewardship and modern
permaculture, this discipline views community as a living
system, like a garden, requiring care and balance. Shared
rhythms of work and rest weave connection, supporting
the eudaimonic cycle's communal aspect.

The Unfinished Bridge of Pontia

In the city of Pontia, which spanned a dark, slow current known only as the River of Perpetual Debt, there stood a bridge of such peculiar and persistent construction that its story merits examination. It was built of granite, rising not to challenge the sky but only enough to let the barge of Memory pass beneath it.

Its distinction was its perpetual, unfinished state: every citizen, from the child whose hand grasped his father's belt to the oldest man who moved with the slowness of stone, was bound to carry one single, unpolished block to the bank each morning. No more, no less. This was the measure of their life.

The bridge was not merely structure but a living boundary. Its arches hosted nests woven from the River's own mud; the granite at its base yielded sharp, dark berries for the children; and at its center, a smoking torch burned not against the night, but against the fleeting light of day. When the brutal, inevitable storms cracked the piers, the townsfolk mended together, their collective labor a shared practice of repair drawn from the stones of their daily practice.

A casual observer, an engineer perhaps, weighted by the hurried tallies of distant cities, would calculate the bridge's mathematical terminus and find it always recessed exactly two human lifetimes into the future. He left Pontia bewildered, having sought efficiency and finding only ritual duration.

Yet for the townsfolk, the rationale was clear, if unwritten: the bridge endured, secured not by a grand original design, but by the silent, unyielding demand of the canal itself. It was the task, not the structure, that held the city together. And the townsfolk knew, with a certainty that settled in their bones, that the day the bridge was truly Finished, the city of Pontia would vanish, having exhausted its reason for being.

Dog Taste Test

Lhasa laps souchong
A bitter tongue dance a wary eye glanced
And
Nudges away the bowl.

Fox (a poem)

Smoke smell
Fire but through and not near
enough to trust the meter
Not near enough to hear the banter

I wait
Skirt
Perimeter pacing
Padding
Observe
remember my approach in twilight
Wait
Pace

Dusk and dawn
Alone and drawn
Slightly out of sight

For now
Tonight

Away

The Town of the Inverse Harvest

In the settlement of Aretè, the citizens worked not for the coming harvest, but for the harvest after the harvest that came next. This was their law, inherited from the first stone placed on the ridge.

They planted their communal terraces with seeds genetically tuned to patience, whose true yield was always delayed by two seasons. When the sun ripened the current grain, it was the bounty of their grandparents' foresight, not their own toil. Consequently, no man felt pride in the basket he carried today, for he had not sown it; his pride lay only in the small, unburdened seeds he had dropped into the earth for a grandchild he would never meet.

The true measure of prosperity in Aretè was never the grain stored in the silo, but the Size of the Fallow. A virtuous year was one where so much had been consciously and communally left untouched—a wild border of unfelled wood, an aquifer never tapped, a meadow reserved only for the bees—that the inhabitants felt a haunting certainty: they had succeeded by the measure of what they had not required.

On the longest night, the elders would gather and tell the children of the Holes in the Map—the spaces where their own immediate desire had been deliberately subtracted from the territory. They claimed that when the communal virtue was truly high, one could sometimes hear, from the deepest, most unnecessary thicket they had chosen not to cut, the sound of the future harvest growing backward into the earth.

It sounded, they said, exactly like breathing.

Light Spark Crisp

Light
Spark
Crisp scratch sound and splinter
Next
Rusted
Connection
a
Precise
Articulation
Gone to
Must and
Fall
Feathered lichened mossy paths of
Familiar nowhere wandering
Dappled leaf and
Storied thoughts of
Warmer clothing
Common companions
Patterns now
In
time's design

I wonder why I keep wearing mittens at
such an advanced age

on Permaculture and Communal Stewardship

Community grows through steady, shared returns.

Relationships, like gardens, need patient tending.

Mutual care turns isolation into fertile ground.

Shared rhythms align hearts and hands.

Presence yields the richest harvest.

Giving and receiving build resilience.

Small acts—watering, listening—sow deep roots.

Stewardship begins with joining the story.

Connection thrives in cycles, not demands.

A community's strength lies in its pauses.

Section VIII: The Tangible World
Discipline: Wabi-Sabi
Craft & Material Devotion

Rooted in Japanese *wabi-sabi,* Zen carpentry, and Depression-era folk repair, this discipline celebrates imperfection through hands-on making. Crafting with wood, clay, or thread grounds you in the eudaimonic effort phase, fostering patience and presence.

It's not about flawless outcomes but honoring the material's nature and your own grounded care.

The Mapmaker's Daughter

In the port city of Itero, every surface bore the patina of movement—salt from the departing ships, dust from the arriving caravans, the arithmetic of trade pressed into the pores of its bricks. It was a city perpetually in transit, forever measuring itself against horizons.

From this restlessness was born a mapmaker, and from him, a daughter named Silvana, who inherited not his charts or his calculations, but a single, confounding instrument: a compass whose needle did not point north, nor to any known pole, but always toward a place within Itero that was being forgotten.

These were not secret places, merely ones that had slipped from notice. A patch of sun-warmed dust behind the fish market. A small, perfectly smooth stone buried beneath the bank. A shuttered attic window that had not faced the sea in years.

The compass led her there, and she obeyed, not as a pilgrim but as a listener. She neither swept the dust nor unearthed the stone nor unlatched the window. She only stood, poised in a stillness that seemed to match the quiet breath of the place itself.

Soon she was known, half in jest and half in awe, as the Keeper of the Zero-Value Spaces.

The merchants dismissed her as a curiosity, for their eyes were trained on distant coasts, their hands charting the routes of exchange. To them, Itero was a ledger written in stone and sea, every street a line of profit connecting somewhere else.

Yet beneath this hum of commerce, the city began to change.

In the patch of dust, a flower took root—no seed planted, no hand tending—and it never wilted. Beneath the bank, the stone began to weep a slow, cooling moisture, a balm for the fevered city air. And the closed attic window became the resting place for migratory seabirds, who paused there, briefly, before resuming their infinite arc.

These places were too small for the eye of record-keepers. No decree marked them, no offering was laid. But a sweetness entered the wind. Tempers cooled. Trade balanced itself without quarrel.

Itero prospered, though no one could say why. Its prosperity arrived softly, like a tide returning to a shore it had once abandoned.

No citizen traced this grace to the girl who lingered in forgotten corners, attending to what the world refused to count.

For what Silvana had preserved was not space, but attention itself—the slender thread between existence and neglect.

In time, the compass was found again, lying in the shadow between two market stalls. Its needle spun slowly, then stopped—not toward any point within Itero, but toward a direction that could not be followed, a place beyond all measure, where the forgotten things of the world go to rest.

And those who held it swore they could hear, faintly beneath the ticking of the ports and the counting of the coins, the sound of a girl's quiet breathing—steady, patient— as if the city itself were still being watched over.

Wander
Leave one task unfinished.
Walk without checking the sky.
A leaf may offer what the screen never could.
Some signs aren't posted.

The Builder of Found Things

During a winter of such lean
proportions that it scoured the very
hills, a man began to build. His
materials were not quarried stone or
fresh-cut timber, but things the world
had deemed finished: weathered planks
bleached by sun and rain, crooked
nails bent from forgotten tasks, bricks
heavy with moss from fallen walls.
He polished each salvaged bit with
a deliberate gentleness, studying its
unique flaw, and placed it with a care
that transcended mere construction.

His neighbors, accustomed to the
conventional order of new materials
and grand designs, watched with a
quiet skepticism. "It won't hold," they
muttered among themselves, observing
the mismatched timbers and the uneven
lines.

Yet, it did. The cabin stood.

Years later, travelers passing through
the valley would speak of it. Long before
they crossed its threshold, or felt the
warmth of its small hearth, they would
sense, unmistakably, that this humble
dwelling felt like shelter. Its form,
assembled from what was discarded,
projected an enduring quality, a silent
testament to the care that had bound
its disparate parts into an unexpected
whole.

on Wabi-Sabi Craft and Material Devotion

Craft reveals meaning in the act, not the finish.
Imperfection is life's honest mark.
Honor materials, and they steady you.

Slow hands learn what haste overlooks.
Making is care between hand and earth.
Beauty grows in worn edges and cracks.
Humble work anchors the heart.
Each scratch tells a story of touch.
Repair restores more than things.

**Make something
modest**

Section IX: Attention & The Digital Drift
Discipline: Digital Silence & Focused Creation

Drawing from monastic silence, Indigenous storytelling
pauses, and hands-on tech like microcontroller
programming, this discipline reclaims attention from
digital noise.

Alternating silence and creation anchors the eudaimonic
cycle's rest and effort phases, turning tools into
instruments of presence and care.

The Boy Who Found His Shadow

A boy lived in a world of light—the blue wash of screens, the blinking rhythm of alerts. His attention scattered. He stopped noticing things.

One afternoon, in the quiet of a library, he found a note tucked inside an old book. It held only a riddle: "Find your shadow again."

Puzzled, the boy returned to his grandfather's house. One by one, he turned the screens off. The silence that followed was strange, almost loud. He sat in it, resisting the urge to fill the space. In that stillness, his senses changed. He noticed the weight of his breath, the wind in the trees, the soft tick of the wall clock.

With time, his curiosity returned—not for noise, but for making. He began building small machines of his own design. They blinked only when he told them to. They served, rather than summoned.

His dog, a gentle giant named Barley, had always known him as a figure washed in flickering light. But now Barley watched as the boy's hands moved with quiet purpose—twisting wires, fitting pieces, shaping order. The constant glow was gone. In its place: the click of tools, the hum of presence.

Barley would rest his head on the boy's knee, as if to say: *This is better.* And it was. The boy, once adrift in a current he couldn't feel, had found rhythm, shadow, and self.

Barley

Barley was a Newfoundland, vast and soft, his paws heavy with the weight of quiet, his fur like drifting shadows that softened the edges of the world. He was born into a universe already humming with hidden measure: planets circling, tides folding, light bending in invisible patterns. At first, the noise of it all overwhelmed him— wind, water, the stir of leaves—but slowly he discovered the silence between sounds, the space where order waited to be noticed.

In this stillness, Barley began to sense a pattern. A dust mote drifted in a sunbeam and paused just so; a shaft of light stretched across the floor and lingered; the air trembled with delicate harmonies. All of it moved according to a measure beyond his understanding, a divine rhythm that had existed long before he drew breath.

Barley learned to align with it. He did not command, he did not shape; he only chose where to rest, when to breathe, which movement to make. And the world responded—not by changing, but by revealing its beauty. Shadows curved with grace. Sunlight traced golden diagrams across the tiles. Even the dust, tiny and ordinary, spun in elegant, unhurried arcs.

Each act of attention—pausing, listening, resting—was an echo of the greater pattern. When Barley moved in harmony with it, the universe revealed itself: a note struck just in time, a drifting leaf guided by unseen hands, air flowing in gentle, deliberate eddies.

Barley was not a god. He was a Newfoundland, vast and patient. His joy came not from mastery, but from recognition: the quiet happiness of knowing his choices were aligned with the flow of creation, that his presence allowed the invisible order to shine.

Sometimes, from his broad, low vantage, he could see it: shafts of light bending over tiles, the shimmer of air caught in motion, the precise curves of dust tracing its orbit. It was as if the universe itself paused to breathe, waiting for him to notice. And when he did, it shimmered in response: light arced a little brighter, shadows curved a little softer, and the air itself seemed to hum a quiet, jubilant chord.

Barley's life became a meditation in movement and stillness. Each breath, each pawstep, each attentive pause was a prayer, a note in the infinite music of the cosmos. Through him, the divine order did not need to assert itself—it simply resonated, reflected, and shone.

And when he rested at last, enormous and serene, his head heavy on his paws, his eyes half-closed, the world itself seemed to rearrange in gentle accord: the stars above bent slightly to mirror his alignment, constellations shifting with quiet joy, a comet lingering in a perfect curve, as if the cosmos itself were sighing, delighted that one creature, patient and attentive, had found its place within the divine pattern.

Barley was entirely happy. Entirely aligned. Entirely home.

on Digital Silence and Focused Creation

Attention is your truest
wealth—guard it.

Silence builds presence
where noise fragments.

Focus is freedom won
from distraction.

Tools serve when
wielded with care.

Creation turns digital
drift into purpose.

Stillness reveals the
mind's quiet rhythm.

A machine's pulse can
steady the hand.

Choose what to ignore to
find what matters.

Pause to hear the world
beyond screens.

Attention shapes life
more than speed.

Section X: The Shape of a Life
Discipline: Hedgerow Building and Maintenance

Rooted in ancient land stewardship, hedgerows—living boundaries of shrubs and trees—nurture and define.

This discipline sees life as a hedgerow: shaped by care, pruning, and growth.

It reflects the eudaimonic cycle's balance of effort and renewal, fostering stewardship and openness.

The Traveler and the Hedge

A traveler, hollow from endless
seeking, came to Robert
Branch, the Hedgemaster,
and asked for a map. Robert's
hands, gnarled like roots
and thick with the memory
of seasons, hovered over the
living hedge. He offered her a
simple tin whistle instead.

"A map will lie," he said. "Life
is not a line. It is a rhythm.
It is the shaping of a hedge,
the weaving of growth, the
gathering of what waits to be
noticed."

At first, the traveler could only
make thin, sighing notes from
the whistle. Her hands, trained
for ink and paper, trembled
as she cut the hedge with a
billhook that seemed too sharp,
too alive. Thorns tore at her
skin, but Robert taught her the
invisible measure: the slow
breath, the deliberate swing,
the tender insistence of living
wood.

Days passed. Sunlight and
shadow measured themselves
against her patience. The hedge
grew not as a barrier but as
a lattice of small universes:
branches weaving, leaves
spinning, air drifting in delicate
arcs. The whistle's notes rose
and fell, and she realized they
were not separate from the
hedge, nor she from them.

Each melody, each cut, each pause was a movement in a single, vast rhythm.

Time no longer flowed for her; it spiraled. Each breath she drew echoed in the branches, each note resonated in the leaves, each careful swing of her hands reshaped the hidden geometry of the living fence. She understood: she was a node in the hedge, and the hedge was a node in her, and both were notes in the same endless melody.

One evening, when the sun had fallen into the horizon like a gold coin tipping over, she rested her hands against the hedge, the whistle humming between her fingers, and whispered, "This hedge lives—and by tending it, so do I."

The world paused to answer. Light curved through the branches with a little more grace. Shadows aligned themselves in delicate, fleeting patterns. A single leaf trembled as if it had learned to breathe. In that instant, the hedge, the whistle, and the traveler were no longer three things but one: a small universe singing the hidden music of care, patience, and presence.

And she, at last, understood the rhythm of existence: life is not a map, not a line, not a path. Life is a melody, and she had learned to play it.

on Hedgerow Building and Maintenance

Life thrives
at its tended edges.

Boundaries grow
with care, not force.

Pruning shapes
as much as planting.

Wild tangles
hold unexpected life.

Steady care
builds a
living fence.

A hedge shelters
yet
opens to the world.

Legacy grows
through seasons of
tending.

To shape life
is
to
embrace
its

flow.

Growth needs structure
        and freedom both.

Patience
weaves
boundaries
into

life.

Author's Note

I do not believe that novelty is a virtue. What's rare isn't what's new—it's what endures. Rhythm, attention, good work, silence, humility—these aren't fashionable, but they are trustworthy. I've come to value what's well-made, quietly kept, and honestly lived.

This book is not a doctrine. It's a field guide. A way of remembering what the body and the world already know: that effort and rest are not opposites but partners; that presence is not a mood but a practice; that our days are shaped less by ambition than by small, steady choices— when to rise, what to eat, how we speak, where we give our care.

If there's any wisdom here, it's not mine. I've read widely, wandered often, and made every mistake twice. But I've been fortunate to read good books, to live in the company of some very nice dogs, a very smart lady, a lot of books and trees and plants, and to return—again and again—to the clarity of a broom-swept floor, a simmering pot, a well-written sentence.

There's a certain kind of wisdom that only arrives after you've tried every shortcut and paid several times and ways for each one. If I've written anything useful here, it's not because I'm clever, but because I ran out of patience for cleverness. I was never one to chase novelty for its own sake, but now? I trust what's simple, durable, and quietly made. The good life isn't hidden. It's just hard to notice when you're in a hurry.

This rhythm—effort and rest, presence and pause—isn't mine. It belongs to nature, to craftsmanship, to older ways of living that weren't trying to be impressive. It's something you feel when you're kneading bread or mending a fence. It doesn't shout. But it holds.

We were never meant to be abstract. The world is already spiritual. It doesn't need our commentary—it needs our participation. That's what this book hopes to offer: a nudge back to the real. Something honest, something useful. Something you can practice.

If you're still looking for how to live, I'd suggest: learn to make something. Fix a drawer. Bake a forgotten type of bread or an odd, historic potpie. Grow an edible Chinese or Victorian vegetable from seed. Read old books. Rebel by being clean, fit, cultured, mannered, and friendly. Schedule time for no-schedule time. Show up. Try to love. Practice mercy on yourself and others.

That's religion enough for a lifetime.

How to
Light a fire
Bucket down in garden earth and must
and rust and hopeful mourning
With molded grasses damp
no urgent hurried need ahead
save dewy chilly lingered cobwebs
and soon
a cattle bell and dog
The latter waiting to be fed

How to strike the match
And start the day
away
from memories of lesser
more complex and thoughtless ways

How to boil the kettle
And wait the moment
Removed from flame
When genmaicha or powdered mush-
room does
Remind
There is more to do
And little time
More to do than sit and rime the rise away

A tail slaps the floor expectantly

Further Reading

Practical Craft and Self-Reliance

The Whole Earth Catalog (1970s editions)
An inspired compendium of tools, ideas, and
philosophies that celebrate self-reliance and
hands-on engagement with the world—perfect for
anyone seeking to cultivate skill, independence, and
thoughtful simplicity.

**The Mother Earth News, issues from the first
five years**
Practical wisdom for living closer to the land, these
early issues championed the rhythms of nature,
sustainable work, and community—echoing the
eudaimonic balance between effort and rest.

Beard on Bread – James Beard
Mastery in the kitchen as a form of mindfulness and
craft, exemplifying how everyday work—like baking—
can be a form of meditation and self-respect.

Back to Basics – Reader's Digest Association
A straightforward manual of practical skills,
celebrating the dignity of self-sufficiency and the
grounding power of good, honest work.

Raising Poultry the Modern Way – Leonard S. Mercia
A feed-splattered handbook with no illusions about mud, mites, or hard winters, yet still suffused with the quiet satisfaction of tending something fragile into thriving, day by day, coop by coop.

How to Build Animal Housing – Carol Ekarius
From chicken tractors to goat sheds, this is a barn-scented catalog of care—practical, sturdy, and full of respect for the creatures we shelter and the humble structures that weather storms with us.

The Tool Book – Phil Davy
Not a metaphor in sight—just a loving inventory of every clamp, chisel, and plane, each with its purpose and dignity, reminding us that good tools—and knowing how to use them—are a form of grounded grace.

Clock Repairing as a Hobby – Harold C. Kelly
An unexpectedly tender manual, where each escapement wheel and mainspring becomes a meditation on patience, precision, and the beauty of making old things tick again—one measured tick at a time.

The Woodburner's Companion – Dirk Thomas
A warm and crackling guide to splitting, stacking, seasoning, and burning—celebrating not just the fire itself, but the slow rituals of tending it well, through blisters and frost and satisfaction.

Eric Sloane's America – Eric Sloane
An illustrated meditation on the ingenious everyday: windmills that turned the sky into labor, canal boats that moved goods with patience, and barns raised by hands that knew timber, weather, and community—reminding us that the old ways weren't quaint; they were brilliant.

All Creatures Great and Small – James Herriot
A tender, mud-splattered ledger of life among animals and their people, full of cold barns, warm hands, small triumphs, and the humbling reminder that healing—like living—rarely goes to plan, but is worth doing anyway.

Spiritual Foundations and Inner Life

The Imitation of Christ – Thomas à Kempis
An early-modern devotional classic that calls the reader to humble interiority, steadfast patience, and the sanctification of everyday tasks through quiet discipline.

The Everlasting Man – G.K. Chesterton
A spirited defense of the Christian narrative and human vocation, reminding us that the rhythms of work, rest, and presence are part of a larger story of creation and redemption.

The Seven Storey Mountain – Thomas Merton
A luminous spiritual autobiography chronicling the journey from wandering to rootedness, exemplifying the monastic rhythms of stillness, labor, and faithful presence in the world.

The Practice of the Presence of God – Brother Lawrence
A quiet call to integrate the sacred into simple daily acts, teaching that presence and purpose are found not in grand gestures, but in the humble rhythm of ordinary life.

Philosophy, Poetry, and the Natural World

The Razor's Edge – W. Somerset Maugham
A narrative exploring the search for meaning beyond worldly success, reminding us that growth is an inner journey as much as an outward striving.

Essays – Ralph Waldo Emerson
An invitation to find the divine in the natural world and in individual effort—championing self-trust, purposeful work, and the cycles of growth and rest.

The Book of Tea – Okakura Kakuzo
A poetic meditation on simplicity, ritual, and the beauty found in mindful presence, aligning well with the cycle of deliberate effort and contemplative rest.

Riprap – Gary Snyder
Poetic explorations of nature and the self, blending the practical and the spiritual in a way that honors the rhythms of life and the deep interconnectedness of all things.

Zen and the Art of Archery – Eugen Herrigel
An exploration of how mastering a physical art like archery opens the door to deeper understanding of Zen principles, illustrating the harmony between mind, body, and the moment of effortless action.

Technology, Environment, and Society

Technics and Civilization – Lewis Mumford
Not a Ludditic screed, but a carefully argued history of technology's cultural shaping force—drawing attention to how tools, rituals, and sacred rhythms have been displaced by efficiency and abstraction.

A Pattern Language – Christopher Alexander, Murray Silverstein, and Sara Ishikawa
This book offers a practical framework for creating spaces that nurture human flourishing—reminding us that growth happens not just inside, but in the environments we build and inhabit.

And Lastly

Thank you for reading. Now close the book. There's work to do.

And, that's a good thing.

www.ingramcontent.com/pod-product-compliance
Lightning Source LLC
Chambersburg PA
CBHW020755130626
46554CB00006B/2204